P9-CLC-028

The Arts

MIKHAIL BARYSHNIKOV

rourke biographies

The Arts

MIKHAIL BARYSHNIKOV

by

ALECIA CAREL TOWNSEND

Rourke Publications, Inc.
Vero Beach, Florida 32964

∞ The paper used in this book conforms to the American
National Standard for Permanence of Paper for Printed
Library Materials, Z39.48-1984.

Library of Congress Cataloging-in-Publication Data
Townsend, Alecia Carel, 1969-
   Mikhail Baryshnikov / written by Alecia Carel Townsend.
      p.   cm. — (Rourke biographies. The arts)
   Includes bibliographical references and index.
   Summary: A biography of the former Soviet ballet star
who broadened his career after coming to the United States,
becoming a choreographer, actor, and director of the Ameri-
can Ballet Theatre.
   ISBN 0-86625-484-6 (alk. paper)
   1. Baryshnikov, Mikhail, 1948-   —Juvenile literature.
2. Ballet dancers—Biography—Juvenile literature.   [1.
Baryshnikov, Mikhail, 1948-   . 2. Ballet dancers.]   I.
Title. II. Series.
GV1785.B348T68   1993
792.8'028'092—dc20
[B]   92-42547
                                                     CIP
                                                      AC

PRINTED IN THE UNITED STATES OF AMERICA

Contents

Color Illustrations

The Arts

MIKHAIL BARYSHNIKOV

Chapter 1

The Art of the Dance

Ask Soviet-born ballet dancer Mikhail Baryshnikov what his plans are for the future, how long he expects to keep performing, or what he thinks of life in the United States, and he may hesitate. Ask him about modern dance or Hollywood—quiz him on politics, fatherhood, or superstardom—and to all of these questions, he might respond something like this:

> I just want to say that all my answers are in my dancing. Watch me and you will see what sort of things I think, what sort of human being I am.[1]

For Mikhail Baryshnikov, dancing is the best method of communicating his feelings, his beliefs, even his opinions. Dancing is his first language, his life's work, and his ongoing contribution to art and our society.

An Artist Called Baryshnikov

Mikhail Baryshnikov is one of the greatest dance artists of our time. Baryshnikov initially achieved fame as a ballet dancer. However, his accomplishments cross over into many kinds of dance, leading him to discover the many extraordinary ways that movement and emotion blend into dramatic art. Today, he continues to explore new possibilities for expression through dance. His desire to learn all that he can from other great dancers is one thing we can admire and learn from him. His exceptional talent, ability to master a variety of dance styles, and breathtaking performances are all significant contributions to our society.

What Is Ballet?

Ballet (*bahláy*) is much more than tights, toe shoes, and tutus, much more than mirrors and music. Like any language, ballet has a specific vocabulary. Its five basic positions and numerous steps are combined to create a dance, just as letters and words are combined to create a sentence. Being able to understand complicated sequences of steps is sometimes referred to as "dance intelligence."

Ballet dance is based on structure and discipline. It uses movement that is unlike normal, everyday movement. Ballet dancers strive to suggest lightness with each step and extreme height with each leap. This is managed, in part, by constant attention to *turn-out*, the outward rotation of the hips. Turn-out is what makes extensions of the leg, deep *pliés* (knee bends), and *pirouette* turns (turns on one foot) possible. However, because turn-out is so unnatural for the body, it is not easy to achieve.

Because these steps can be highly technical and difficult to perform, a ballet dancer must be in extremely good physical condition. The dancer is also an athlete. In addition to the steps, ballet often expresses emotions, so the dancer must be an actor, too. Mikhail Baryshnikov is all of these things: a dance scholar combining steps, an athlete surpassing normal physical limitations, and an actor invoking emotion in his audience.

Like any other art, dance attempts to record some aspect of life. The art of dance creates images in movement that help the audience to become more sensitive to reality, even after the movement's image has faded. However, dance is different from other art forms because the dancer's instrument for communicating these images is his or her own body. A painter uses paint and canvas, a composer uses a piano, and a sculptor uses clay. A dancer like Baryshnikov uses his own body to realize his artistic vision.

12

Mikhail Baryshnikov at age twenty-six, shortly after he defected from the Soviet Union.
(AP/Wide World Photos, photo by Dina Makarova)

The images created through dance have the potential to offer insight into aspects of our culture and the time and place in which we live. As a dancer, Baryshnikov has the opportunity to communicate insights about our world as well as to entertain and amaze audiences with his artistry.

How Did Ballet Begin?

Baryshnikov works within many *genres*, or types, of dance, but his first love is the ballet. Ballet is one style of dance. It began in Europe hundreds of years ago as an expression of elegance and grace, and later as a way of telling stories. In France, Italy, and Russia, untrained dancers performed in the courts of kings and queens. Gradually, the skills needed for ballet dancing became more difficult, and by the 1830's ballet dancing was considered a profession.

Ballet developed in different ways depending upon the country in which it was performed and the artistic directors who helped guide its progress. These artistic directors usually included a *choreographer*, who created and arranged the dance steps; a *composer*, who wrote the music for the ballet; and a *librettist*, who wrote the story or plot that was going to be told through dance. Costume designers, set designers, rehearsal leaders, and theater officials were also often involved in these productions.

Many important developments in the art of ballet dance took place in Russia, Baryshnikov's homeland. One significant event occurred many years before his birth in 1880, when the Russian czar invited a French ballet master named Marius Petipa to teach in Russia. Instead of making ballet *divertissements* (or short movement "diversions" without a complicated plot), Petipa began to create full-length ballets that told a story. Petipa emphasized *virtuosity*, or skill, over elegance. He devised very precise choreography for the dancers. His "classical" ballets, which include *The Nutcracker* and *Swan Lake*, are still performed today.

After many years, another Russian dancer, Michel Fokine, expanded on Petipa's vision to suit the talents of increasingly skillful dancers. Decades later, in 1948, Baryshnikov was born into this long tradition of dedication to the dance. Like his ballet forefathers, Baryshnikov has continued to revise and perform these classical ballets for new audiences. Most important, Baryshnikov was instrumental in bringing elements of this rich Russian tradition to American stages. His heritage and training are Russian, but he is cherished by audiences in the United States and throughout the world.

Baryshnikov as the Prince in ABT's production of The Nutcracker. *The still popular classic ballet was, in the 1880's, one of the first full-length ballets choreographed.* (AP/Wide World Photos)

A Man of Many Talents

Baryshnikov has mastered more than ballet technique. He has also explored other dance styles, including modern dance, tap dance, and jazz dance. Since settling permanently in the United States in 1974, he has studied and collaborated with leading figures in these various genres of dance. He has even performed in a Broadway play and appeared in several movies.

Baryshnikov constantly seeks new challenges, believing that they offer him freedom. Until the end of the Soviet Union in 1991, freedom was limited in Russia and artistic opportunities were strictly monitored. Because he grew up in such a restricted environment, Baryshnikov has always cherished the freedom he finds on the stage. In reflecting on his life's work, Baryshnikov says:

> Every ballet, whether or not successful artistically and with the public, has given me something important that I could store up for future use. . . . Everything that I've done has given me more freedom. It's like learning many new languages, all of which expand one's flexibility and range. The dancer, just like the language scholar, needs as many as possible. There are never enough.[2]

The dance has given Baryshnikov the chance to be free, and in return he reveals to his audience an unmatched artistry. Both in his performances and in the story of his life, we can find the freedom that is the art of the dance.

Chapter 2

Growing Up in Russia

Baryshnikov was born on January 27, 1948, in Riga, the capital of Latvia, one of the former republics of the Soviet Union. His father, Nikolai Baryshnikov, was a Soviet officer who held traditional Russian political and social ideals. His mother, Aleksandra Kiseleva, was a vibrant, attractive woman who loved the ballet. She often took her son with her to see local productions. As a young boy, Baryshnikov liked sports, particularly soccer. He especially liked being outdoors, enjoying the freedom of open space. When he was eleven, he decided on his own to enter the Riga Dance School.

Getting Started

At first, Baryshnikov's father was not happy about his son's desire to dance, wishing that he would study engineering or aeronautics instead. Already an athlete, Baryshnikov (or "Misha," as his friends call him) soon proved that he had an exceptional talent for the dance. To become a professional dancer, aspiring students usually begin lessons at the age of seven or eight. Though at eleven he was older than most beginners, Baryshnikov learned the basic ballet *vocabulary* (dance positions and steps) with remarkable speed.

After two years, his instructors moved him to an advanced class. There he was required to study mathematics, history, literature, French, art history, and piano at a nearby school. All of these classes were in addition to the rigorous ballet curriculum. Baryshnikov became a favorite among his teachers, who called him "charming," "an inspiration," and were convinced that young Misha possessed a special talent.

Sadly, Baryshnikov's mother never witnessed his emerging talent. Soon after his first dance lessons, she committed suicide. He never knew exactly why, although he realized that she was often unhappy. Her sudden death remains the most tragic experience of Baryshnikov's life.

Comfort in Dance

Besides the absence of his mother, many aspects of life were painful for Baryshnikov and for other Soviet youth of his generation. The political ideology of communism, part of the Soviet way of life, was not as appealing as it was to people of his parents' generation. Many young Russians were disillusioned by the apparent failure of communist ideals. The theory of communism holds that private individuals cannot own property; instead, all goods should be distributed equally among all members of society. Although the majority of Russians believed in these ideals, many were shocked by the ruthlessness of Soviet political leaders whom they once had trusted. The Soviet Union had become a "police state" in which the slightest breaking of a rule would invite harassment and sometimes endanger the "guilty" person's life.

No nation can live under such fear for long. As social and economic conditions in the Soviet Union became worse, people began to rebel against the government's strict rules until, in 1991, the Soviet Union finally broke into many separate countries. Thus, at the very moment that Baryshnikov was training to be the best dancer in the ideal world of ballet, the political ideals of his country were beginning to fall apart.

Ballet offered Misha an escape from the personal and social conflicts that invaded his childhood and adolescence. The drama of the dance allowed him to hide behind the characters he created. The world of the ballet seemed more stable and comforting than the world "outside." Its glamorous costumes and glittering lights helped to mask his emotional pain.

18

Baryshnikov's homeland: Mikhail Baryshnikov was born in Riga, Latvia, which was once part of the Soviet Union (below). He studied dance in Riga for four years before moving to the Vaganova Choreographic Institute in the grand old city of Leningrad (now known as St. Petersburg), pictured above.

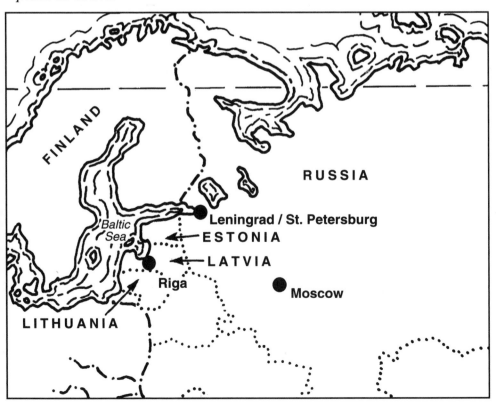

As a teenager, Baryshnikov knew that he wanted to be very good at whatever career he eventually chose. He also knew that to excel at anything requires a great deal of hard work, dedication, and commitment. He quickly devoted himself to becoming the best dancer that he could be, using all of the resources available to him as a student in Russia.

As part of the Soviet Union, however, the Russian government had strict rules about the kind of art that was allowed to be created and performed. The communist ideology upheld by the government until 1991 insisted that all art serve the state and exist under centralized control. Ballet was considered acceptable because of its strong connection to the past—to the "classical" tradition. Unfortunately, according to this ideology, there was very little room for experimentation or innovation.

Finding a Mentor

After four years at the Riga Dance School, Baryshnikov felt ready to undertake greater challenges. In 1964 the Riga dancers went on tour to Leningrad, and young Misha instantly fell in love with the big, cobblestoned city. People who saw Baryshnikov dance in Leningrad that year were startled by his technical skill, his artistry, and his mature attitude on stage. At his teacher's insistence, Baryshnikov auditioned for Leningrad's Vaganova Choreographic Institute in September of that year. This famous ballet school was named after the great Russian dance teacher of the early twentieth century, Agrippina Vaganova.

At the Vaganova Choreographic Institute, Baryshnikov had classes in character-dance, acting, and lifting his partners into the air. Most important, he was accepted into the "classic-dance" class of Alexander Ivanovich Pushkin, who was considered to be one of the last of the great Russian ballet masters in the tradition of Petipa and Fokine. Baryshnikov studied with Pushkin for the next three years. Their friendship, however, remained strong until the older man's death in 1970.

Studying with Pushkin was significant for Baryshnikov. Pushkin became a mentor to his student, guiding both the development of Misha's dance technique and the growth of his inner character. Looking back on his years with Pushkin, Baryshnikov later said, "Everything he gave me is in one way or another the beginning—the solid beginning—of how I now understand it all."[3] Pushkin's guidance affected many aspects of Baryshnikov's life.

Training for Stardom

Pushkin was famous for training the best male dancers—known as *danseurs* (*dahnsóor*)—in Russia. In his classes, Pushkin emphasized dancing according to the logic of the steps. He helped his dancers train their muscles so that the body's "memory" could take over without thinking about the particular sequence of events. Using Pushkin's method, dancers also developed their individuality. Even with identical training, Pushkin's dancers gave performances that were emotionally distinct. Pushkin taught dancers how to convey the drama of the dance using their own personal style.

Pushkin was also famous for his large leaps and powerful jumps. Baryshnikov, already a strong jumper, was encouraged by Pushkin to use his natural coordination to increase the height of his jumps. Large, soaring leaps are essential for male dancers.

Technique was not the only thing that Baryshnikov absorbed from his mentor. Pushkin also taught Misha the difference between dancing in a classroom and dancing on a stage. Baryshnikov remembers when he first learned this:

As a young dancer I had a quite developed, secure technique, but my sense of style was often appalling. It is of the utmost importance to work very hard to make technique and style one.[4]

21

Dancers must be prepared technically to make their entrances on the stage. Once there, however, they must transform their performance into dance—not simply a display of technical skill. Learning the magic of stagecraft was a significant lesson for Baryshnikov.

Pushkin also encouraged his dancers to become intensely focused on their work, helping them to decide early whether they should pursue the humorous, exaggerated "character" roles or the leading-man "virtuoso" roles, which required great skill. Baryshnikov appreciated Pushkin's encouragement, later describing his mentor like this:

> He taught in such a way that the dancer began to know himself more completely, and that, I believe, is the first key to serious work, to becoming an artist—to know oneself, one's gifts, one's limitations, as fully as possible.[5]

From Pushkin, Baryshnikov learned an important lesson: that he, Baryshnikov, was the only person who could *realize* (make real) his own potential. At an early age, Baryshnikov knew that it was up to him to become the best that he could be.

More than technical skill or emotional dynamics, Pushkin gave Baryshnikov an appreciation for learning itself. The young student eagerly absorbed all that he could from this master teacher, including the idea of self-education. Pushkin fostered a respect for all of Russian culture in his young pupil, as well as an unquenchable intellectual curiosity. Unlike most of his peers, Baryshnikov was very curious about contemporary innovations in the arts of Western Europe and North America. This early openness to Western culture would later serve Baryshnikov well. But first, with his training complete, he had bigger challenges at home.

Chapter 3

Star of the Kirov

In 1967, three years after moving to Leningrad from Riga, Baryshnikov graduated from the Vaganova Choreographic Institute and joined the famous Kirov Ballet. To this day, the Kirov remains one of Russia's two most accomplished classical dance companies. (The other, the Bolshoi Ballet, is based in Moscow.) Throughout the 1950's and 1960's, the Kirov's powerful artistic director, Konstantin Sergeyev, worked hard to preserve the Russian classical ballet tradition. Respecting the wishes of political authorities, however, Sergeyev refused to allow innovation or much creativity to find its way onto the Kirov stage.

A Dancer Without *Emploi*

Sergeyev liked Baryshnikov. He felt that young Misha's talent would enhance his own choreography, which some people found dull. Sergeyev realized that Baryshnikov was unique because he did not fit into one particular category of male dancers. Generally, the Kirov insisted that dancers be cast into one of two traditional *emploies*, or styles. The *emploi* was determined by physical appearance, musculature (the arrangement of the muscles), and technical abilities. A male dancer was categorized as either a romantic lead (*danseur noble*) or a character dancer (*demi-caractère*). Female ballerinas were typecast in a similar way. Because separating dancers according to *emploi* was thought to preserve the integrity of the original choreography, dancers did not usually move from one style to another.

Possessing both handsome good looks and a sense of

humor, Baryshnikov was difficult to categorize. He easily adapted to diverse balletic styles, playing both the romantic and the comedic parts with sensitivity and authority. In addition, there seemed to be no limits to Misha's talents. His colleagues at the Kirov were at first jealous and then astonished by his flawless technique. Time after time, Baryshnikov brought new energy to old masterpieces.

Mastering the Permitted Roles

Despite this extraordinary talent, few challenging parts were available to Baryshnikov as a recent graduate from the Vaganova Choreographic Institute. Because he was not yet considered experienced enough for the leading male parts in such famous ballets as *The Sleeping Beauty*, *Giselle*, or *Swan Lake*, he was frequently given roles that did not make full use of his gifts. Most often, he performed in a program that included several *pas de deux*, or duets, by classical ballet choreographers. Not only were these duets overused, but Baryshnikov also lacked a female partner who was good enough to help him revitalize them. While he danced with many partners throughout his time at the Kirov Ballet, none of them ever quite matched his amazing artistic abilities.

Baryshnikov spent the next six years at the Kirov mastering the classical ballet roles and struggling for the freedom to experiment with new ones. In 1969 he danced the part of Mercutio in a new staging of William Shakespeare's romantic story *Romeo and Juliet*. He astonished the audience with his high-speed combinations, intricate lifts, and rapid rotations in the air. To his dismay, the ballet was banned after only one performance. The Artsoviet, an official committee that determined Kirov policy, believed that this production threatened conventional morality because of its passionate love scenes and was inappropriate for the Russian stage.

By his third season with the Kirov, Baryshnikov had

become a star. The Soviet public loved him, and some even considered him to be a hero. This recognition meant that he received a salary about four times greater than the *corps de ballet* (*core de bahláy*), or body of dancers (the French word *corps* means "body"). Stardom also ensured Baryshnikov a place in the company's tour of London in 1970. This was Baryshnikov's first glimpse of the West, and Western critics' first glimpse of Baryshnikov. Both sides were very impressed.

In addition, stardom brought several original roles created by various choreographers for Baryshnikov. A *choreographer* is a person, often a dancer, who creates or arranges steps and puts them together to make a dance. Leonid Jacobson, an unusually innovative choreographer, created the ballet *Vestris* for Misha in 1969. Auguste Vestris was an eighteenth-century French dancer famous for his mime technique; he often amused (and sometimes annoyed) members of the royal court with his caricatures. Performed for an international ballet competition held in Moscow, Baryshnikov's *Vestris* was boldly theatrical. Misha won a gold medal for this performance, and he later restaged the dance for American audiences. For someone who liked challenge as much as Misha did, dances such as *Vestris* did not come around often enough.

A Fight for Individuality

In 1971 Baryshnikov danced in a new ballet called *The Creation of the World*, staged by Bolshoi ballet masters and based on satires of biblical stories. The Bolshoi Ballet allowed new ideas to be tried more often than the Kirov, and so *Creation* evolved into a sophisticated, entertaining work. As the curious, youthful Adam, Baryshnikov won the approval of any who had previously doubted his abilities as an actor. After *Creation*, the only thing left for Baryshnikov to prove was his ability to dance in the classic lead roles.

One year later, Baryshnikov gave his debut performance of

A look at classical ballet: A good example of classical ballet is Giselle, *created in 1841 in Paris. Baryshnikov made his debut at the Kirov in a pas de deux from* Giselle. *Later, he perfomed the lead male character for his American Ballet Theatre debut (above) on July 27, 1974, with Natalia Makarova (left). As a classical ballet from the Romantic era,* Giselle *tells a story through dance. The nobleman Albrecht, engaged to be married to another woman, falls in love with a peasant girl named Giselle. Despite their passion, he betrays Giselle by going ahead with his arranged marriage. She dies, brokenhearted. Later, Giselle's spirit forgives Albrecht and saves him from the revenge of the Wilis, ghosts of maidens who have been deceived by love. Albrecht is a technically and emotionally demanding role. The character's motives are open to interpretation by the dancer. Baryshnikov, while acknowledging the importance of the female lead, described the part as an "unequaled dramatic opportunity for the male lead.* Giselle *can, in fact, be a two-person drama, and it is the acting that makes the part of Albrecht such a great challenge."* (Baryshnikov, *Baryshnikov at Work*, p. 26)

Albrecht in *Giselle*. The part of Albrecht is very demanding, and it is danced only by the greatest male dancers. Once again, Misha triumphed in this role, giving it a new interpretation that showed a different side of the character's emotions. In addition, his success in this role finally refuted the Kirov's sacred notion of balletic *emploi*: Baryshnikov had proved that he could master any dance style, not just one. Misha was ready for more.

Creative Evenings

Many Kirov dancers, including Baryshnikov, longed for the chance to create and perform new choreography. Others wanted the opportunity to demonstrate their skills in roles not usually offered to them. A partial cure for this frustration was found in the idea of "creative evenings." These shows usually presented a series of short pieces or one-act ballets. The productions were organized by an individual dancer, who was given the freedom to choose the dancers and choreographers with whom he or she would work.

Hoping to prevent any new trends or styles in dance from interfering with the classical tradition, the management allowed each "evening" to be presented two or three times only—and sometimes just once. As could be expected, some evenings were more successful than others.

Baryshnikov was assigned an evening in early 1974. He welcomed the chance to work with new choreographers, especially those who did not have the government's official approval. Along with this small freedom, however, came the responsibility to prove his worth not only to an adoring public but also to the ever-watchful company administrators. Baryshnikov spent the entire winter season of 1973-1974 preparing for his creative evening, pouring heart and soul into his original work. He decided to ask several unconventional choreographers to compose dances especially for him. His production was going to include three new ballets—a rare occurrence at the Kirov.

Disappointment

Rehearsals for his production did not go as Baryshnikov had planned. Some dancers were unwilling to spend extra time practicing, some were unwilling to be part of the cooperative process of choreographing new dances, and some brought personal problems with them onto the stage. Baryshnikov went home night after night discouraged, wishing for more dedicated and enthusiastic colleagues. As opening night approached, nothing connected with his creative evening seemed to be working, from the set construction to the colors of the costumes to the steps themselves.

Despite these technical problems, Baryshnikov's creative evening was significant for the Soviet audience. He proved to them that even in a country where art was censored, such as Russia, the individual creative spirit can still survive. Tickets for his performances quickly sold out.

Members of the Artsoviet were not as inspired, however. They harshly criticized Misha's presentation, revealing their dislike for those who had the courage to try new ideas. After the performances were over, Baryshnikov became even more unhappy about his work at the Kirov. One friend remembers him saying, "I tried my best. It's not my fault that I joined the company when it was falling apart."[6]

A Chance to Escape

Dissatisfied with the way his career was progressing, Baryshnikov longed for a change. Watching him perform, another friend wisely remarked, "When Misha is ready for freedom, his frustration will prompt him to make the right decision. He will leave Russia. . . . Remember my words."[7]

This friend's prophetic statement came true later that year.

In the spring of 1974, Baryshnikov was again selected to go on tour with the ballet company, this time to Canada. It would be his first trip to North America. As fate would have it, this was also good-bye to his homeland.

Chapter 4

Good-bye to Homeland

Canada, June 29, 1974. *Baryshnikov paced back and forth inside the home of a friend. His plan to escape from the watchful tour leaders was complete. The legal preparations had been taken care of earlier that week. All that remained was Misha's final, irrevocable decision to seek citizenship in the United States.*

Soon it was time to leave for his evening performance at the theater. Baryshnikov tried desperately to hide his nervousness and fear. If the tour leaders thought that something was amiss, they would immediately remove Baryshnikov from the group and he would probably never get another chance to travel to the West.

That night, in his last performance with Soviet dancers, Baryshnikov was brilliant. The audience's applause thundered through the hall. Because of a malfunction with the set, however, the performance had been delayed, and Baryshnikov was on stage later than he had planned. Then, after the performance, the tour directors told him that a car would be waiting at the backstage door to take him to a farewell party. These complications could put his escape plan in jeopardy.

He raced to his dressing room, changed his clothes, and dashed for the exit. Fans and admirers swarmed at the door, clamoring for autographs and handshakes. He pushed through the crowd and managed to reach the sidewalk. He started running, shouting over his shoulder that he was going to say good-bye to some acquaintances and would be right back.

Darting among cars as he raced down the street, Baryshnikov finally met his waiting friends. They pushed him

*into a taxi and took him to safety. That night, Baryshnikov
requested formal political asylum in Canada. Later there was
a celebration marked by both excitement for things to come
and sadness for things left behind.*

Why Leave Russia?

Even as a star, Baryshnikov had become increasingly aware
of the serious problems surrounding him in Russia. Though he
had chosen a glamorous profession, everyday life in the Soviet
Union was very difficult. Material goods such as clothing and
housewares were scarce or extremely expensive. Often, there
were shortages of food. People would stand in lines for hours
at a time waiting for bread or meat, especially before the long,
bitterly cold winter months began.

Unlike the U.S. government, the Soviet government
supported the nation's ballet dancers by providing them with
salaries and shelter. This was helpful for the dancers, but it by
no means made a luxurious lifestyle possible. The popular
dancers in the Soviet Union did not accumulate the kind of
wealth that famous artists often achieve in the United States.
When Baryshnikov was beginning his career in the 1960's,
dancers received very small salaries—only about $200 per
month. The majority of them could not afford cars or their own
apartments. They lived in communal housing, sharing a living
space with other family members or complete strangers. In
some cases, as many as twenty families would share a large
apartment with only two bathrooms. Baryshnikov was
extremely fortunate to have been given a comfortable
apartment all to himself.

A Chance to See the World

The lives of Russian dancers were further complicated
because of the demands and rules that the government

31

Baryshnikov with Dina Makarova, arriving in New York less than a month after his defection. (AP/Wide World Photos)

enforced upon their careers. In the former Soviet Union, dancers did not have the freedom to pursue their careers in the way that American artists do. Generally, their progress and choices were carefully managed by the government and the Artsoviet.

For example, Russian dancers were not allowed to leave the country. It was well known in the Soviet Union that those who defected, or left the country without permission, would be subject to a minimum of fifteen years in prison if they dared to return or were caught. Perhaps if Baryshnikov had been allowed to study abroad for short periods of time, he might not have sought a permanent home in North America.

The exceptions to this rule were government-sponsored tours, such as the trip that brought Baryshnikov to Canada. Foreign tours were important to the dancers because they received bonus pay and a chance to return to the Soviet Union with such luxuries as jeans, heavy jackets, and shoes. They could sell these items at home in order to buy cars or larger apartments.

Dancers competed intensely for the opportunity to go abroad and were careful not to offend the theater officials or local politicians, because that might hurt their chances of being chosen. The Russian secret police, known as the KGB, carefully watched the dancers being considered for travel. Not until the day of departure did KGB guards post a list of the dancers who had been chosen to go. Changes in the cast were possible right up to the plane's take-off. The KGB wanted to prevent defections like Baryshnikov's.

A Chance to Excel

Although the Russian lifestyle was difficult, economic realities were not the main reasons behind Baryshnikov's decision to leave his homeland forever. Friends in Russia realized that his talent, though widely worshiped, was being

33

wasted in Leningrad. French choreographer Roland Petit even said about Baryshnikov, "With his fantastic talent, sitting around at the Kirov is simply suicide—he'll choke on the routine."[8]

Baryshnikov seemed hesitant about taking the risk to leave, but he was clearly considering it. The heartache that had accompanied his "creative evening" had stayed with him. That same year, he asked his good friend Gennady Smakov if he thought he could find success in New York. Smakov replied, "I guarantee you that in a couple of months you'd be a superstar." As it turned out, Baryshnikov became a superstar after only a few performances with American Ballet Theatre that summer.

Misha's friends back home in Leningrad were stunned at the announcement of his defection. Some loyal fans were so distraught that they, too, considered leaving the Soviet Union. Rumors ran wild through Russia about what really happened that night in June. At first the government, wanting to prevent embarrassment and scandal, said that Baryshnikov had been given official permission to study abroad. In time, government leaders omitted his name from Russian history books, deleted his image in television and movie productions, and destroyed performance programs with his name on them. However, his close friends soon heard news of his tremendous success in New York, and they knew that he had made the right decision.

Chapter 5

The Leap to ABT

Many new experiences awaited Baryshnikov in New York, which is home to two of the United States' largest ballet companies: American Ballet Theatre (ABT) and the New York City Ballet (NYCB). Each company had its own style, traditions, and resident choreographers. Over time, Baryshnikov would become acquainted with both.

America Responds

While still in Canada, Baryshnikov contacted Natalia Makarova, a principal ballerina at ABT. They had been friends and dance partners in Russia before she chose to defect in 1970. When Makarova heard of Baryshnikov's decision to stay in the West, she arranged for him to be her partner again. Makarova knew that the best place for Baryshnikov to prove himself was at ABT, because this company regularly performed the classical ballets at which he was so proficient. Their first performance together in the United States would be in *Giselle.* Tickets, already scarce because of her scheduled appearance, sold out immediately when it was announced that the young genius from Leningrad would be appearing with her.

On July 27, 1974, twenty-six-year-old Mikhail Baryshnikov made his debut on the American stage. The critics and audience were thrilled by his perfect technique, his breathtaking leaps, his incredibly fast *pirouettes* (turns), and the intricate steps which he would execute without hesitation or noticeable preparation. By the end of the summer, Baryshnikov's name was recognized in households across the country.

Baryshnikov helps fellow defector and famous dancer Natalia Makarova celebrate her thirty-ninth birthday. (AP/Wide World Photos)

In the spring of 1975, dance critic Marcia B. Siegel saw Baryshnikov perform on several occasions with American Ballet Theatre. She later described his technical achievement:

> He can do more beats, more complicated footwork, faster turns than any male dancer I've ever seen. Some of his most dazzling steps result from his ability to change the position of his legs or upper torso right in the middle of a jump or a turn. He's not a large man, yet onstage he gives you the impression of covering vast distances. . . . [9]

On another occasion, Siegel summarized the total impact of Baryshnikov's artistry: "This is one time when all the blurbs are true—you have never seen dancing like this; it simply hasn't been done."[10]

A Time of Transition

Despite this public success, the progression from the Kirov stage to American Ballet Theatre was not easy. The abundance of personal and artistic opportunities was overwhelming to Baryshnikov, as it was for many Russians who move to the West. In the Soviet Union, an individual's actions were generally dictated by the government. Suddenly, Baryshnikov found himself able to make choices for his future. Along with this freedom, however, came new responsibility for his decisions—an unfamiliar and sometimes uncomfortable pressure. (One of those difficult decisions came later, when Baryshnikov left American Ballet Theatre for the New York City Ballet.)

Baryshnikov was glad to have the friendship of Natalia Makarova, who made an excellent partner for him. Makarova, too, was pleased that Baryshnikov was dancing with ABT, because he was a link to her homeland as well as a brilliant artist. Baryshnikov also caught the attention of Gelsey Kirkland, one of America's greatest ballerinas. Baryshnikov and Kirkland formed a memorable partnership that lasted several years, as did their romantic involvement offstage. (The break-up of their personal relationship was very painful for both of them, however, and received a great deal of publicity.)

Building His Repertoire

With great enthusiasm, Baryshnikov tirelessly pursued new ballets to add to his *repertoire*, or collection of dances. Between 1974 and 1976, Baryshnikov danced a total of twenty-six roles—a very high number for any ballet dancer in such a short period of time. Almost all of these parts were new to him, making his accomplishment doubly astonishing. He even had the chance to travel, performing in such places as London, Greece, Rome, Paris, and Australia. He frequently made guest appearances with London's Royal Ballet and the National Ballet of Canada.

As one of American Ballet Theatre's most popular stars, Baryshnikov danced in the classical ballets night after night. He performed the lighthearted *Les Patineurs* (the skaters) and the comedy *La Fille mal gardée* (the poorly watched daughter) with just as much ease as he did the tragic *Petrouchka*, the story of a puppet confined by his strings and tormented by love. Misha's flawless Russian training and finely tuned body made him a natural for the leads in *Giselle* and *Swan Lake*.

Baryshnikov had long since mastered these familiar characters. He knew them inside and out, and they always drew a large audience. Gennady Smakov remembers Baryshnikov saying:

> We've already danced *Giselle* so many times that for me each new performance is a special sort of recollection. The body's memory almost subconsciously draws out of somewhere some nuances, which in essence are not really new at all. They have already been done.[11]

A "special sort of recollection" is the way Baryshnikov describes his mastery of classical ballet. His words also

A look at contemporary ballet: Push Comes to Shove *is a good example of a contemporary ballet. Unlike a Romantic ballet, such as* Giselle, Push *does not tell a story. Rather, it conveys ideas in a more abstract way. Choreographed in 1976 by Twyla Tharp,* Push *poked fun at traditional, classical ballet conventions—while remaining an extremely technically difficult ballet. With a background in modern dance (a discipline that evolved during the early twentieth century in America), Tharp used movement differently from the way a ballet choreographer would.* Push *became a huge hit, and also one of Baryshnikov's greatest challenges.*

Tharp used several techniques to "spoof" the classical ballet tradition. References to well-known sections of classical ballets were interwoven into the choreography, so that the dance parodied what the dancers themselves revered. The timing of the steps was not precisely with the music, which was an unusual mixture of ragtime and classical. Often the choreography purposely threw Baryshnikov off-balance. Baryshnikov described his first encounter with Tharp like this: "In classical ballet I more or less know what the possible is, but in this case I had no idea what I could or couldn't do. Twyla pushed me and encouraged me to accomplish many things I never would have dreamed I could do." (Baryshnikov, *Baryshnikov at Work*, p. 189)

suggest that, in spite of his stardom, he was always ready for a new challenge.

Pushing the Limits

Baryshnikov found relief from the classical routine in more contemporary Western ballets, such as Roland Petit's bleak ballet about death entitled *Le Jeune Homme et la mort* (the young man and Death). Another significant addition to his repertoire was the difficult *Theme and Variations* by George Balanchine, who was one of twentieth-century America's greatest choreographers. In his ballets, Balanchine emphasized

Kirkland and Baryshnikov in ABT's production of Tchaikovsky's The Nutcracker. (AP/Wide World Photos)

patterns, shapes, and choreographic construction over drama. Baryshnikov was eager to grasp the Balanchine style because of its appeal to a dancer's intelligence, not simply his emotions.

Another choreographer who emphasized structure and form

was Twyla Tharp. As a modern dancer, her creation of *Push Comes to Shove* for Baryshnikov and ABT in 1976 was especially significant. Before this collaboration, ballet dancers and modern dancers had purposely stayed away from each other. The two dance forms were considered incompatible. Tharp and Baryshnikov disproved this common sentiment. Baryshnikov also experimented with jazz dance, performing in Alvin Ailey's *Pas de Duke* with Judith Jamison. For this dance, he was asked to leave his ballet slippers at home—quite a sacrifice for a classical dancer.

The Challenge of Choreography

Two other Russian defectors, Makarova and Rudolf Nureyev before her, had "re-staged" several Kirov ballets for ABT. Acting as directors, they instructed the company in the choreography and specific mannerisms that they had learned in the Soviet Union. Baryshnikov, too, was given this opportunity.

In 1977, he directed the ever-popular classical ballet *The Nutcracker* for American Ballet Theatre. While this ballet was already familiar to Americans, Baryshnikov made noticeable changes, looking back to the original choreographer (Petipa) and composer (Tchaikovsky) for new clues to the production. This version of *The Nutcracker* was filmed for television that year, and it is often aired during the Christmas season. Next, Baryshnikov turned to the slapstick romantic comedy *Don Quixote*, which he had danced many times at the Kirov. Baryshnikov's version, which placed ballerina Gelsey Kirkland in the leading role of Kitri, premiered in March, 1978, in Washington, D.C.

Response to these productions varied; some critics felt that he had made too many changes. Baryshnikov himself considered these ventures to be part of the learning process. As it turned out, he was right: His first years at American Ballet Theatre were just the beginning of a multifaceted career.

Chapter 6

The Jump to NYCB

With the mastery of the classical roles, the staging of two large productions, and an enticing taste of modern choreography behind him, Baryshnikov believed that it was time for another dramatic career change. In the fall of 1978, he moved his home base—from American Ballet Theatre to the New York City Ballet. To some, this crossover was a surprise. It was rumored that Baryshnikov was shifting his loyalty from one company to the next. To others, however, it was an obvious step for such a brilliant artist. Baryshnikov himself defended the move by stating his desire to work with two important choreographers affiliated with NYCB: George Balanchine and Jerome Robbins.

The Magic of Mr. B

Balanchine represented the ultimate challenge for Baryshnikov. Mr. B (as his dancers referred to him) was born in Russia. Throughout the 1920's he had danced with Serge Diaghilev's innovative company, the Ballets Russes. Like Baryshnikov's, Balanchine's training descended from the long line of Russian and French ballet masters, particularly Petipa. However, departing from the Soviet tradition of Romantic ballets which had formed the basis of Baryshnikov's training, Balanchine created dances without plot or story. He focused on the patterns made by groups of dancers moving together and the various combinations of steps, spins, and jumps within the ballet vocabulary. This approach to choreography, which stresses form over content, is called *neoclassical*.

For someone as adept at conveying emotion and drama as

Baryshnikov, in costume for a perfomance of Coppelia, *pauses to talk to choreographer George Balanchine.* (AP/Wide World Photos)

Baryshnikov was, Balanchine's more impersonal mode of performing required much effort to learn. Balanchine even approached the basic dance steps differently from Baryshnikov's teachers in Russia, so it was necessary to learn a new technique as well as a new style. In tackling Balanchine's choreography, Baryshnikov was taking another look at his entire ballet heritage.

The results of this collaboration with Balanchine were mixed. Several factors made the work difficult. For one thing, Balanchine typically featured the ballerina rather than the *danseur* in his ballets. The male roles were less developed than those designed for the female. Therefore, Baryshnikov's talent for sustaining a mood throughout the dance was wasted. In addition, Balanchine preferred to make the focus of the ballet the *corps*, or group of dancers, rather than singling out any "stars." Accustomed to center stage, Baryshnikov had to learn to blend his individual style into that of the group.

Juggling Roles

From July, 1978, to October, 1979, Baryshnikov intensively studied the *repertory* (a selection of dances performed regularly) of the New York City Ballet. For the first six months, he was rehearsing more than fifteen Balanchine ballets at once. In all, he performed twenty-five new roles during his stay with NYCB.

With his eye for new opportunities, Baryshnikov relished even the exhausting, endless rehearsals that this undertaking demanded. In November he appeared in Balanchine's *Rubies*, performed on the opening night of NYCB's 1978 season. The ballet combined classical movements with elements of jazz technique, such as bent knees, sharp turns, and rotations of the hips. For this combination to be successful, the dancer had to perform the steps without adding any emotional overtones. This was nearly impossible for Baryshnikov, who portrayed the role in the Russian manner—with added characterization and humor.

Baryshnikov had greater success with *The Prodigal Son*, one of Balanchine's masterpieces, created in 1929 and based upon the biblical story. (Balanchine's earlier ballets, like this one, more directly reflected the Russian tendency toward storytelling.) Still, some critics found fault with the level of emotion that Baryshnikov brought to the title role. His dancing was also compared to an earlier, memorable portrayal of the Prodigal Son by another superstar, Edward Villella.

Apollo, re-created by Balanchine during the spring of 1979, gave Baryshnikov a second chance to succeed at Balanchine's impersonal style. This time, Baryshnikov concentrated on the abstract characteristics of the movement itself. The emotional impact that Balanchine desired came more naturally out of this concentration on the technique.

La Sonnambula was one of Baryshnikov's favorite ballets by Balanchine. A romantic tale about a poet and his dreams, this ballet offered Baryshnikov a role that was primarily one of pantomime. Here, the use of his natural emotional instincts and acting abilities was appropriate to the theme of the dance.

Although his experience at NYCB was not always easy, Baryshnikov gained much through the study of Balanchine's ballets. He later wrote:

> I can't say enough about what it's like to work with Balanchine and to dance his ballets. . . . Maybe a simple statement is the best answer: Balanchine is a genius; his masterpieces are incomparable; and that's that.[12]

Fancy Free

If Balanchine offered Baryshnikov a reevaluation of his Russian heritage, the great Broadway chroeographer Jerome Robbins presented him with a new definition of the American

As Apollo in George Balanchine's ballet of the same name (1983). (AP/Wide World Photos)

tradition. Without doubt, Robbins has significantly contributed to twentieth-century dance with his spirited choreography. With a flair for the dramatic and his eye on contemporary jazz and theatrical dance, Robbins typically takes his inspiration for the movement from the music he has chosen.

Like Balanchine, Robbins can be classified as a "neoclassical" choreographer. That is, in his work he attempts to redefine the traditional Russian, classical ballet style. The ballet technique—the steps—remains the same. It is the application of this technique that has changed. Robbins adds elements of jazz, modern, and Spanish dance, as well as common, everyday gestures, to his ballets. For example, Robbins is remembered for choreographing the exciting dance sequences in the musical *West Side Story*, in which two rival gangs take their violent feuding into the streets.

Baryshnikov had worked with Robbins once before. In 1976, Robbins had choreographed a one-act ballet called *Other Dances* especially for Misha and Makarova. The ballet had no story but was instead a series of solos and duets inspired by the lyrical, romantic music of the nineteenth-century composer Frédéric Chopin. Baryshnikov described the experience like this:

> Working with Jerry was a complete revelation. Sometimes he would take a rehearsal and dance the whole thing for me; I wouldn't dance a step. But seeing him dance is what brought me closest to dancing it the way *he* wanted. He gave so much that I learned it all more quickly than I thought I would.[13]

Baryshnikov performed *Other Dances* again when he was with the New York City Ballet, but this time with a different partner. Unfortunately, some of the poetry of the dance was lost with the change in casting.

One of the most memorable dances by Robbins is *Fancy Free*, a one-act jazz ballet with music by Leonard Bernstein.

Fancy Free is a lighthearted look at three sailors on shore leave who cannot wait to impress the girls. Each sailor takes his turn in a show-off solo that reveals aspects of his personality. Baryshnikov danced the role of the Second Sailor in 1979.

Other dances by Robbins that Baryshnikov performed during this period included *Dances at a Gathering* and *Afternoon of a Faun*. Robbins also choreographed two dances specifically for Baryshnikov: *Opus 19* and *The Four Seasons*.

Struggle Against Time

Because of the strenuous work that all dancers do, day after day, their performing careers tend to peak early, usually when they are in their twenties. By the time he resigned from NYCB, Baryshnikov was thirty-one years old. He had effectively prolonged his youth by undertaking so many challenges. He had mastered the classical Romantic style of his homeland and had tackled the abstract, neoclassical style of the incomparable Mr. B. Misha had also proven himself to be a charming entertainer in the uniquely American ballets of Jerome Robbins. This preparation was necessary for Baryshnikov to assume an even more difficult role: Artistic Director of American Ballet Theatre.

1. The young Baryshnikov. (AP/Wide World Photos)

2. A state-run department store in Riga, Latvia, Baryshnikov's birthplace.
   (Jeff Greenberg, Unicorn Stock Photos)

3. A view of St. Petersburg, Russia (formerly Leningrad), where Baryshnikov studied at the Vaganova Choreographic Institute. (Frank Siteman, Lightsources)

Star Quality

Nina Alovert, a photographer and writer born in Russia, chose to defect from the Soviet Union to the United States of America. First, however, she saw Baryshnikov dance in his graduation recital at Leningrad's Vaganova Choreographic Institute in 1967. Bored by the preceding presentations, Alovert quickly became alert when Misha made his entrance in the pas de deux *from the ballet* Don Quixote. *She remembered her first impressions of Baryshnikov the student: "Not only was the professionalism and purity of his technical execution rare for a graduating student, but his high and beautiful jumps were incredible. . . . He was not the interpreter of movement; he himself was movement. . . ." She asked dancer Alexander Minz about Baryshnikov, and he replied, "Remember his name; you'll be hearing more about him."* (Alovert, *Baryshnikov in Russia*, p. 25)

At right, Baryshnikov is seen rehearsing for Don Quixote *with the famous ballerina Natalia Makarova in 1974.* (AP/ Wide World Photos)

5. Baryshnikov performs with the Martha Graham Dance Company in her ballet *American Document*, 1989. (AP/Wide World Photos)

6. In rehearsal with the Martha Graham Dance Company, 1988. (AP/Wide World Photos)

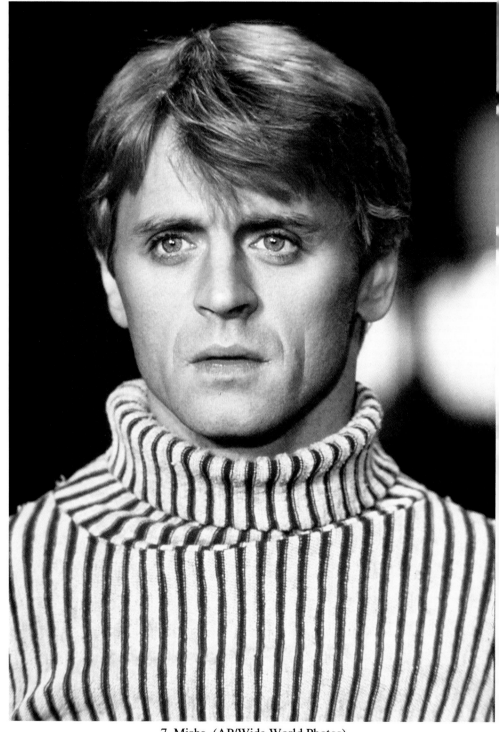

7. Misha. (AP/Wide World Photos)

8. Dancing with Natalia Makarova. (Robert McElroy, Woodfin Camp and Associates, Inc.)

9. Rehearsing for *The Metamorphosis*, the story of a man who awakens one day to find himself transformed into a beetle. (AP/Wide World Photos)

10. Baryshnikov and fellow actors are coached by director Steven Berkoff during a rehearsal for *The Metamorphosis*. (AP/Wide World Photos)

11. Performing on television with Liza Minnelli in *Baryshnikov on Broadway*. (AP/Wide World Photos)

12. Baryshnikov poses with his colognes. (AP/Wide World Photos)

13. Baryshnikov escorts two models who are wearing "Baryshnikov Bodywear." (AP/Wide World Photos)

Chapter 7

Turning Points

When the chance to manage one of the world's largest ballet companies was offered to him, Baryshnikov saw before him a new kind of challenge. The artistic director of any performing group has immense responsibilities: from instruction and choreography to long-range planning and fund-raising. Under the leadership of Lucia Chase and Oliver Smith since 1945, American Ballet Theatre had grown to a company of eighty-seven dancers with a repertory of seventy-five ballets. Misha would take control of a large and complicated organization.

As he had already learned by staging *The Nutcracker* and *Don Quixote* for ABT, directors and performers have very different jobs. This is how he described that difference:

> Once you are the stager of a ballet, or the director, you have to abandon all hope of the responsibility of belonging to anyone but yourself. *You* pick the dancer, *you* pick the designer, *you* pick the form. And then the curtain goes up and the responsibility is yours, all yours.[14]

As Artistic Director, Misha would make decisions that would determine the success or failure of the entire company.

Baryshnikov also realized that a great benefit might result from this increased responsibility: As the director of ABT, he would have the chance to blend the best of his Russian ballet training with the freedom for creative expression that he had found possible in America. He saw an opportunity to bring the two traditions together:

I know that the company's tradition of having a wide and varied repertoire of works from all over the world in all styles must be maintained. I also hope that I can bring a renewed sense of the classical style to the company and that it will continue to grow and prosper.[15]

Looking back, Baryshnikov would later see that this goal posed enormous challenges for him.

ABT Gets a New Director

Baryshnikov assumed the role of Artistic Director of American Ballet Theatre on September 1, 1980. The date marked the beginning of a turbulent decade in his career, filled with new experiences—some satisfying, some frustrating. This period brought Misha sharp criticism for the first time, often coming from the same people who adored him on stage.

From the moment the announcement of Baryshnikov's directorship was made, ballet-watchers expressed serious doubts about his qualifications for the job. In fact, it was assumed that he had been offered the position simply because he was a celebrity. No one questioned Baryshnikov's genius as a performer, but some people wondered if his administrative skills could possibly match his artistic skills.

Critics also worried that it was inappropriate to let a Russian-trained dancer manage what was begun as a distinctly "American" company. Baryshnikov's appointment therefore suggested an interesting twist, summarized in May, 1980, by critic Walter Terry:

The first company to be founded expressly for the promotion of American dance will be led by a dancer trained in the most disciplined of Russian traditions.[16]

Others worried that Baryshnikov would overemphasize the Russian style or spend too much time reworking the classics at the expense of supporting newer dances. The company itself

At the Kennedy Center in 1986, ABT Director Baryshnikov strikes a dramatic pose.
(AP/Wide World Photos)

worried that he might show favoritism to Russian dancers.

Baryshnikov, like all superstars, also had a much-publicized reputation that was not always based on fact. He frequently was featured in tabloids and entertainment magazines that wanted to promote a glamorous image of him. They often portrayed him as a playboy, a jet-setter, or a self-serving artist. His romances with other dancers or actresses always made the headlines. As Artistic Director for ABT, he was watched even more closely.

Baryshnikov's Revolution

Only six months after assuming his position, *Newsweek* magazine called the striking changes at ABT "Baryshnikov's revolution." Several significant events had occurred.

First, Baryshnikov put the dancers through three long months of rehearsals—quite a luxury for a company that earns much of its livelihood by touring. Second, he fired two of the company's stars, Gelsey Kirkland and Patrick Bissell, for constantly arriving late to the company's rehearsals. He then had to confront the larger problem behind their lateness: Both Kirkland and Bissell suffered from serious drug addictions, which frequently impaired their ability to work. As Artistic Director, Baryshnikov had the difficult task of trying to bring these dancers to an adult awareness of their problem. "Leading dancers must set an example to everyone else. . . . For the dancer, the theatre must be a church," Baryshnikov said in one interview. From the beginning, he demanded professionalism and discipline from his dancers. (Baryshnikov would later show great sadness for the loss of a wonderful talent after Bissell was found dead in his apartment from a drug overdose in 1987.)

Misha provided an important example for the dancers himself. One company member described it like this:

When Misha made a correction. . . . I believed him. All I had to do
was look at him and I could see the truth of what he was telling. It
was as if he proved his point every time he danced.[17]

This kind of expert coaching led to a successful first season
beginning at Washington's Kennedy Center. A
seventeen-week national tour followed. Critics agreed that
Baryshnikov had accomplished remarkable things with the
corps de ballet, making them more polished, more unified, and
more central to the productions.

Baryshnikov also demonstrated what one critic termed "a
new accent on youth." After firing Kirkland only twenty-four
hours before opening night, he replaced her with an unknown
eighteen-year-old *corps* member named Susan Jaffe. Her
partner was Bolshoi Ballet defector Alexander Godunov. Their
surprisingly dramatic performance was praised, as was
Baryshnikov's emerging policy to give the lower-ranked
dancers opportunities to prove themselves in front of an
audience. Under Baryshnikov, ABT's long-standing emphasis
on "star power" and seniority was diminishing. As one *corps*
member said, "Misha gets people off their rear ends. At
practice he says, 'Whoever does this step best gets the role.'
He means it."[18]

Choreography was another area on which Baryshnikov
focused. For example, he introduced more ballets by
Balanchine to the company's repertoire, and he revised some
of the full-length classics for which he himself was famous.
Over the next decade, he staged new versions of *Giselle* and
Swan Lake, based on the Russian traditions of his childhood.
The Sleeping Beauty and *Romeo and Juliet* were produced as
well. He also encouraged company dancer Clark Tippet's
interest in choreography, which led to the creation of several
significant works for ABT.

In addition, Baryshnikov commissioned or acquired new

works by contemporary modern dance choreographers, including many famous ones: Paul Taylor, Merce Cunningham, David Gordon, Mark Morris, and Twyla Tharp. He spent time studying with modern dance pioneer Martha Graham and introduced her choreography into ABT's repertoire. These experiments with modern dance offered an interesting new direction for the ballet company. In fact, with their 1990 performance of Graham's *Diversion of Angels*, American Ballet Theatre would become the first ballet company to present Graham's work.

There were other adventures for ABT under Baryshnikov's leadership. On several occasions ABT's productions were filmed for the television series *Great Performances*. For example, ABT's dancers performed *Push Comes to Shove* for a special called "Baryshnikov by Tharp" in 1984. Also that year, the full-length *Don Quixote* was broadcast. In 1987, ABT's production of David Gordon's fantasy ballet *Murder* aired on the *Dance in America* series. Members of the company also appeared in Baryshnikov's 1987 motion picture *Dancers*.

Troubled Times

By 1985 there were signs of trouble in Baryshnikov's revolution at American Ballet Theatre, and perhaps the problems could be traced back even further. The company did not consistently achieve the financial and critical success that it had gained at first under Baryshnikov's guidance, and he grew restless with the routine of board meetings and fund-raising. The large ballets he created were expensive and not always well received. For instance, *Cinderella*, choreographed by Baryshnikov and Peter Anastos together and premiering on December 20, 1983, cost nearly $1 million to produce and was all but forgotten after only one year of performances.

Because of his desire to explore other avenues in his own career, Baryshnikov turned over the day-to-day operations of

ABT to his two associates: John Taras, formerly of NYCB, and Kenneth MacMillan from London's Royal Ballet. Baryshnikov himself appeared at company rehearsals and performances less frequently. In order to have more freedom for projects outside the company, he also gave up his salary and contract for serving as Artistic Director. Each year, he made a "gentleman's agreement" with the company—his continued guidance in exchange for a dollar bill and a handshake.

The 1986-1987 season was critically important for American Ballet Theatre. Controversy surrounding Mikhail Baryshnikov's appointment as Artistic Director was finally fading after five long years, and he was counting on this chance to show off his well-trained dancers, polished choreography, and emerging company style. Still, he was feeling the pressure of several difficult issues and inevitable new controversies, both from inside the company and from unexpected sources outside.

To begin with, the cast list went up for the making of his new movie, *Dancers*. Company members who were not chosen to go to Italy for the filming became angry and jealous. This did not help his image among the group, nor did former partner Gelsey Kirkland's recently released autobiography. In her book, *Dancing on My Grave*, Kirkland painted Misha as an abusive and dominating man, and her tales were so detailed and intimate that it seemed as though no one could repudiate them.

Baryshnikov tried to ignore these obstacles while he planned the year's lavish production schedule in tribute to one of ABT's founding members, choreographer Antony Tudor. He invited Sir Kenneth MacMillan, the newly appointed Artistic Associate, to restage the nineteenth century classical ballet *The Sleeping Beauty*. MacMillan, however, was diagnosed with throat cancer halfway through the ballet's

The conflict over Misha's resignation: In June, 1989, Baryshnikov announced to his dancers that he would be leaving American Ballet Theatre the following summer. He is seen below with former First Lady Betty Ford (left), Martha Graham (center), and Liza Minnelli (right)— during this period. Baryshnikov's reasons for resigning: continuing conflicts with upper management over his freedom in hiring and budgeting, and the extent to which he was responsible for raising money. The tension over these business matters became unbearable for Misha, and he decided it was time to move on. Company dancers were stunned. The year 1990 would mark the fiftieth anniversary of ABT, and Baryshnikov was planning a gala celebration honoring the tradition that he had helped to preserve. It would be a fitting finale to his administrative career. However, on September 28, 1989—months before the gala—he abruptly resigned.

ABT's new Executive Director, Jane Hermann, had unilaterally fired Misha's longtime assistant. This caused an irreparable dispute between Hermann and Baryshnikov. "I'm not taking orders from anyone, especially unfair ones," Baryshnikov said. "I left one country for those very reasons." With that, his nine-year term as Artistic Director ended. The fiftieth anniversary celebration occurred as planned in the summer of 1990, with Misha conspicuously absent. (Anna Kisselgoff, "Baryshnikov Leaves American Ballet Theatre," *The New York Times*, September 29, 1989, p. C7).

creation, so Misha had to take over. More than $1 million later, the company was ready to dazzle its audience.

Aurora, the leading ballerina role in *The Sleeping Beauty*, was to be danced by up-and-coming principal star Susan Jaffe. One week before the ballet's premiere at New York City's Metropolitan Opera House, however, Jaffe suffered a serious stress fracture to her left ankle and had to hang up her toe shoes for the season's duration.

As if these misfortunes were not enough to put the company on edge, on the eve of the New York opening, Antony Tudor died—in the midst of ABT's revival of some of his best-known works. His death followed on the heels of the death from cancer of his colleague, dancer Nora Kaye (who was also a founding member of ABT and whose husband, Herbert Ross, was the director of the film *Dancers*). The beloved popular entertainer Fred Astaire passed away within that same time period.

The combination of these historic deaths made American Ballet Theatre's dancers understandably sad, but none as much as their leader. Misha was asked to announce Tudor's death before the curtain rose on opening night. At first (and to everyone's dismay), he refused. For a man of deep feeling, this request was one too many. Rallying to his duty, however, Misha paid Tudor a loving tribute.

Obviously, such events "cast a pall." The 1986-1987 season was not off to a very good start.

Branching Out

In 1988, Baryshnikov invited modern dancer Twyla Tharp to join ABT as another artistic associate and resident choreographer. This was a positive step in Baryshnikov's revolution, since it represented a unique merging of two genres in dance: ballet and modern. Some of the dancers previously in Tharp's own company came with her to ABT, making this merger even more exciting.

Still, not all of Baryshnikov's administrative actions were considered as valuable as this one. By 1989, the company was operating at a deficit of $1 million. Baryshnikov was criticized for being absent from the stage; the public missed seeing him perform. Issues like this made him a controversial director. Overall, however, Baryshnikov gave American Ballet Theatre the polish and inspiration it needed. After a while, he learned to ignore his critics:

> I really don't care about people's misconceptions. . . . I'm very happy with that peace, that I got to the point where I truly don't care. [The critics] can be very patronizing when they don't like something; they're very much into your policy matters and private life. My idea is to run the company the way I know best. . . . I'd like to be responsible for my decisions.[19]

During this time, Baryshnikov had numerous ventures away from ABT. Movies, television, dramatic theater, and even social causes kept him from being a full-time manager of the company. He had also become a father: Daughter Aleksandra, whose mother is actress Jessica Lange, was born in 1981.

For Misha, it was extremely important to find peace amid these many new roles. By 1989, peace with his position at ABT was impossible. He resigned suddenly, in an atmosphere of turmoil and bitterness.

Chapter 8

A Move to Modern Dance

In his ongoing search for choreographers who could stretch the limits of his incredible talent, Baryshnikov moved away from traditional ballet and collaborated with modern dancers on several occasions. These collaborations have been successful learning experiences for Baryshnikov and important events in the history of dance. Baryshnikov is skillful at using new stylistic devices within the different dance genres; he is also known for adding his own dramatic flair to anything that comes his way. He proved these abilities early in his career, when he charmed audiences in Twyla Tharp's *Push Comes to Shove*. Later collaborations with Tharp and with two additional, very distinct modern dancers—Martha Graham and Mark Morris—have been equally thrilling.

Misha and Martha Graham

Known as an American dance pioneer, Martha Graham is credited with developing a new dance technique. She started dancing in the early part of the twentieth century and had enormous influence on the development of *modern dance*. In fact, her technique was initially a response, or an alternative, to ballet technique—and that is one reason it was called "modern" when she (and several others) began their work. Because Graham's technique was so different from ballet, it was a challenge for Baryshnikov and an achievement for him to learn it.

Although modern dance has been an important form of American twentieth-century art, it was all but forbidden in the Soviet Union while Baryshnikov was growing up. In fact, he was taught that Graham's dances contradicted the Russian artistic ideal because they were not always "uplifting." Graham's choreography typically depicted an individual's exploration of his or her emotions. Sometimes these depictions dealt with very strong negative as well as positive feelings, and they were represented with extremely graphic dance movements.

The first time Misha saw a Graham dance was after his defection in 1974. He remembers being disappointed, because her dancing was not strictly entertaining:

> I was not ready for the ecstatic exaltation of her work. I wanted to be entertained and I found it was not entertainment, it was very much an emotional involvement for the viewer. It took me some time to get into this rhythm. It's a theatre of a unique kind.[20]

Soon, however, Baryshnikov became eager to study the Graham style himself.

Misha and Martha Graham became friends in the late 1970's, when she would occasionally stop by his dressing room after his performances. They would chat about dance, each asking the other about training, technique, and philosophy. "You could say anything you liked to her, a silly joke, and not even think twice," Baryshnikov said in an interview after Graham's death in 1991. "She made me feel the comfort of just being me."[21]

A New Language

Baryshnikov made his first guest appearance with the Martha Graham Dance Company in 1987, while he was Artistic Director of American Ballet Theatre. He played the role of the just-married husband in Graham's famous work *Appalachian Spring*. First choreographed in 1944, this dance depicts the relationship of a young couple to their pioneer community, to their newly constructed frontier home, and to

Among the elite of the dance world in 1987: Maya Plitsetskaya (far right), Rudolf Nureyev (arm around Plitsetskaya), and ninety-three-year-old Martha Graham. (AP/Wide World Photos)

each other. The dance emphasizes gestures: At one point, for example, Misha as the husband symbolically touches the door frame, suggesting a powerful connection to this place and its creation. Each gesture is heavy with meaning but open to interpretation. This is radically different from ballet, in which gestures normally have specific, known meanings.

In 1989, Baryshnikov performed with Graham's company in *American Document*, which was inspired in 1938 by the statements of American writers and political leaders. He also studied the leading roles in both *Night Journey* and *El Penitente* (the penitent one). For Baryshnikov, studying the Graham repertoire was like learning a new language altogether. While some critics believed that he was not as effective as dancers trained from the beginning in the Graham technique, Graham herself was content: "I feel he gives new life and animation to many of my ballets," she said.[22]

For this reason, Baryshnikov was made an honorary member of the Martha Graham Dance Company. He danced without pay at Graham gala performances, and he introduced Graham's repertory to American Ballet Theatre. When she died at the age of ninety-seven, Martha Graham left instructions that Baryshnikov was to be allowed to learn and perform any Graham dance, free of charge. As a result, Mikhail Baryshnikov has helped to preserve the modern dance art of Martha Graham by continuing to present her work to the public, just as he has helped to preserve the Russian classical ballet tradition.

Misha and Mark Morris

Another dynamic and often controversial figure in contemporary modern dance is Seattle-born Mark Morris. Morris is known for "breaking the rules" in dance, in terms of its content, movement, and music. At first glance, he seems to have little in common with a wizard of classical ballet technique like Baryshnikov. Yet the two are similar in one respect: "We like to dance," Baryshnikov explained. "Both of us." This simple, common ground led to a successful collaboration between two very different artists.

Baryshnikov so admired Morris' choreography that he invited him to create a work for American Ballet Theatre in 1988. The result was *Drink to Me Only with Thine Eyes*, a dance that would become part of the ABT repertory. Over the next few years, Baryshnikov appeared with the Mark Morris Dance Company, which was in residence at the Monnaie Dance Theatre in Belgium from 1988 to 1991. He found working with Morris to be extremely rewarding and provocative: "He puts you into the dance, which is in his imagination," Misha explained.[23]

The White Oak Dance Project

The successful working relationship that Baryshnikov and Morris enjoyed led them to another unusual collaboration: the White Oak Dance Project. In the summer of 1990, they spent two months on the lush White Oak Plantation in northern Florida with seven other talented, hand-picked dancers. The huge estate is owned by dance patron Howard Gilman, also a longtime friend of Baryshnikov. Gilman helped to finance this modern dance group, and he even built a one-million-dollar dance studio for their summer rehearsals. "It was an extraordinary set-up," Baryshnikov remarked. "We were isolated from the world by the beauty around us. At the same time, it somehow produced a lot of energy for work."[24]

The group learned Morris' choreography in preparation for an eighteen-city tour. This tour intentionally encompassed cities that did not often have the chance to host modern dance groups. For this project, Morris created a new ensemble work, *Motorcade*, and a trio called *Pas de Poisson* (*Dance of the Fish*). Baryshnikov was also taught Morris' free-flowing, signature solo entitled *Ten Suggestions*.

Misha and Morris emphatically said that this group was not a "company"; that is, they did not wish to form a long-term commitment or put any boundaries on the repertory or dancers. They were also opposed to any labeling of their work as "classical" or "ballet" or "modern." They hoped to demonstrate that dancing is legitimate and artistic regardless of the "school" in which the performer might have been trained. Both genres of dance require discipline and dedication, and one is not more difficult or more beautiful than the other. "There is just good dancing and bad dancing, good choreography and bad choreography," Baryshnikov said in an interview about the project.[25]

As a member of the White Oak group, Baryshnikov was simply a dancer among other dancers. Unlike the ABT

79

programs, in which he got top billing, here his name was listed alphabetically in the roster of performers. There were no stars and no ranking system—simply dancers, working together because they wanted to work together. Baryshnikov described their purpose:

> Although our careers were very successful individually, we all know how rare it is to find a situation when you have a lot of time to yourself, to your thoughts, to work with a choreographer you admire and at the same time not to belong to one big company. . . . It's very much a family attitude. . . . [26]

The White Oak Dance Project made its debut in October, 1990, in Boston.

The group continued to perform throughout the next year. The tour of fall, 1991, featured an ensemble of fifteen dancers and included the work of several other prominent modern-dance choreographers. Martha Graham's *El Penitente*, danced by Baryshnikov, was one of the eight pieces on the program. By this time, Morris was taking a less active role in the group, although his choreography remained. Artistic decisions were made by Baryshnikov.

The White Oak Dance Project was in large part the result of Misha's creative vision and involvement. It was an extension of his desire to keep experimenting with dance in its many forms and configurations—a desire that led him away from his classical ballet heritage. At this point in his career, he appreciated the free, fresh movement created by choreographers like Mark Morris: "I'm much more excited to see modern dance; there are more surprises," Baryshnikov explained in a 1990 interview. "In modern dance, they are definitely ahead of the traditional classical dance. That's just my opinion, but it's why I'm shifting my focus."[27]

Chapter 9

Leading Roles

Throughout his career, Baryshnikov has been involved with numerous projects that took him into new artistic territory. The dramatic flair he continually exhibits in his dancing has found an outlet in several motion pictures, in television specials, and on the dramatic stage. He is as natural in front of the camera as he is before a live audience. Each new project extends the boundaries of his accomplishments.

Broadway Bound

One of Baryshnikov's childhood dreams came true in 1980, when he was invited to prepare a tribute to Broadway musicals for television. Misha had first seen movie musicals as a child in the theaters of his hometown of Riga. He watched Gene Kelly, Fred Astaire, and James Cagney sing and dance across the screen, and he wanted to be just like them. *Baryshnikov on Broadway* was the Russian dancer's tribute to a uniquely American art form, as well as another artistic challenge for this all-around performer.

The one-hour television special showed Baryshnikov being guided through the wonderland of Broadway by his co-star, singer and dancer Liza Minnelli. The show featured exuberant song-and-dance sequences from many familiar musicals, including *Oklahoma*, *Guys and Dolls*, *Kiss Me Kate*, *The King and I*, and *Ain't Misbehavin'*. Misha and Minnelli were also joined by actress/singer Nell Carter and the entire national cast of the Broadway musical *A Chorus Line*. For each number, Misha impersonated characters that had made these musicals famous. *Baryshnikov on Broadway* was, like most Broadway musicals, an extravaganza of song, dance, and good-natured comedy.

In rehearsing for this production, Baryshnikov had to study two new dance forms: tap dance and jazz dance. These are both used extensively in choreography for Broadway musicals, and they challenged his classical technique in new ways. Tap dance is highly structured and rhythmic, requiring great control over the feet. Jazz dancing is sharp and angular—in complete contrast to the elegance of ballet. Baryshnikov also got to practice his singing, joining Liza Minnelli in such favorites as "Sunrise, Sunset" and "Shall We Dance?"

The best aspect of *Baryshnikov on Broadway* is Baryshnikov himself: It is clear that he enjoyed giving this performance. Clearly, the show symbolized a special personal achievement. He paid tribute to the American performers he had admired since childhood, and so celebrated his own life in the United States.

In the Movies

Baryshnikov's on-screen career has been significant, with roles in several major motion pictures in addition to television specials such as *Baryshnikov on Broadway*. In 1977, he appeared in the film *The Turning Point*, starring Shirley MacLaine, Anne Bancroft, and young ballerina Leslie Browne. The film's plot centers on a ballet company modeled after American Ballet Theatre and shows life "behind the scenes." Baryshnikov was nominated for an Academy Award for Best Supporting Actor for his portrayal of Yuri, a brash, talented, and arrogant *danseur*.

The movie featured wonderful dance sequences performed by Misha and his fellow ABT dancers. In fact, many viewers considered Misha's dancing to be the best aspect of the production. Perhaps more important, Baryshnikov's performance in this film (as in all of his films) helped to

Doing the Charleston with actor-singer Liza Minnelli during the videotaping of a one-hour television special, Baryshnikov on Broadway. (AP/Wide World Photos)

increase the number of people exposed to the ballet, thereby broadening the place of dance in society. This role, like all of his roles, also helped to shatter the myth that ballet is an undignified profession for a young man.

White Nights, released in 1985, was Baryshnikov's next feature film. Tap dancer Gregory Hines co-starred with Misha in this action-adventure movie filled with international intrigue and political drama. The film tells the story of a world-class dancer, Nikolai Rodchenko (Baryshnikov), who defected from the Soviet Union only to crash-land, years later, on a Soviet air base. Hines plays Raymond Greenwood, an American tap dancer who has defected to the Soviet Union in his own political protest. An unlikely pair, the two dancers eventually form an alliance to help Rodchenko escape from Russia a second time.

Like *The Turning Point*, *White Nights* contained many elements similar to Baryshnikov's own life story. The movie's director, Taylor Hackford, purposely wove together the real-life personas of Baryshnikov and Hines and incorporated their respective dance styles. The resulting dance sequences, choreographed by Twyla Tharp, are dynamic and help to build the story's suspense. Not surprisingly, Baryshnikov is given plenty of opportunities to show off his technique. At one point, Rodchenko bets Greenwood that he can perform eleven continuous *pirouettes* (turns on one foot). Rodchenko then executes them perfectly, slowing to a halt after the eleventh rotation.

The 1987 film *Dancers* is another romantic drama based on a ballet company. This fictitious company is on-location in Italy, filming *Giselle*. Baryshnikov stars as a burned-out dancer/director named Tony, who finds new inspiration in a young member of the *corps de ballet*. However, he is not as serious about her as she is about him. The off-stage affair mirrors the ballet's tragic story, as both the young ballerina

As Tony in the film Dancers *(1987).* (AP/Wide World Photos)

and the fictional Giselle suffer from broken hearts.
Baryshnikov's real-life dance partner, Alessandra Ferri, plays
Giselle, while Julie Kent plays the younger girl. Baryshnikov
himself staged the ballet sequences, and his own production
company was involved in the movie's creation.

Company Business was released in 1990. In this adventure
film, Baryshnikov co-stars with actor Gene Hackman. The
story revolves around the Soviet and American governments,
who make a deal to trade imprisoned spies—one of whom is
Baryshnikov. The trade-off becomes increasingly complicated
and dangerous, as the U.S. government is blackmailed for $2
million. An action-packed chase follows. The characters
portrayed by Baryshnikov and Hackman escape with all of the
money.

Baryshnikov's films have received mixed reviews. Some critics have found fault with the films' story lines; some have suggested that Baryshnikov stick to dancing. Even some of his loyal ballet fans and dance critics believed that such film and television appearances were tasteless for an artist of Baryshnikov's caliber. On the other hand, many critics have praised his remarkable versatility and on-screen presence. His ease with the English language is also often noted. Furthermore, few have questioned his ability to convey emotion and drama, no matter what part he is portraying.

Live Theater

Baryshnikov's talent for conveying emotion was important for another challenging role—this time in the live theater. In 1989, Misha played a completely different character as the star of Steven Berkoff's adaptation of *The Metamorphosis*. Written in 1915 by Franz Kafka, *The Metamorphosis* is a bizarre, metaphorical tale.

Baryshnikov portrays an exhausted salesman named Gregor Samsa. Haunted by dreams of his demanding family and customers, Samsa wakes up one morning to discover that he has turned into a beetle. His transformation begins a gruesome, pitiful struggle for a sense of identity and belonging. The bug attempts to hold onto his humanity while those around him react with horror. In the end, rejection by those who no longer recognize him causes the beetle to die.

As Samsa the beetle, Baryshnikov was able to combine his dramatic skills and his modern dance skills in a powerful way. He scuttled about the stage like an insect, on all fours, his fingers wiggling. He hung upside-down on the metal jungle-gym that was used to suggest his room. He even pretended to eat a fly. His performance was so convincing that one critic was prompted to write:

Baryshnikov confirms that he is a born actor who became the greatest dancer of his day. When choosing not to dance, he's a great actor still.[28]

This performance required intense concentration and physical agility. In a given week, Baryshnikov would perform *The Metamorphosis* eight times—an extremely demanding schedule. The play itself was ninety-five minutes long, with no intermissions or breaks. Although the director provided general ideas for the choreography, Baryshnikov expanded the movement and made it his own. He also had many lines of dialogue. In preparation, he studied with voice teachers to become comfortable with speaking and projecting to a live audience.

The Metamorphosis premiered at Duke University in North Carolina. While at Duke, Baryshnikov worked closely with the students in various drama classes. About twenty students assisted with the production of *The Metamorphosis*, from stage management to publicity. Presenting the play first at a university provided an excellent opportunity for the students to work with the famous Baryshnikov; it was also a good chance for the director and producers to experiment with special effects and prepare the actors before going on to New York in early March. Once there, under the bright lights of Broadway, the play broke box-office records and attracted large audiences well into the summer.

So Many Hats

Without a doubt, Baryshnikov accepted these roles in television, film, and theater because they helped to satisfy his longing for challenge and his curiosity about various artistic forms. They have added a dimension to his already astonishing career as perhaps the greatest dancer of his generation. Misha is an "all-around performer" and a role model for those who seek artistic flexibility and freedom.

Most of these projects were undertaken while Baryshnikov was Artistic Director of American Ballet Theatre. These activities contributed to his departure from his "ballet home," sometimes causing friction among company members and onlookers. Yet these activities also kept Baryshnikov challenged and helped to create balance in his life. At the age of forty-one, much of this need for balance and expansion no doubt resulted from his knowledge that the length of his dancing career was limited. In one interview, Baryshnikov explained it like this:

> I don't want to dance the things that I can't do as well as I used to. The big bravura ballets like 'Don Q.' [*Don Quixote*] aren't for me now. I would rather take another chance and do something that stretches me. . . . I know I wear too many hats—so many hats. That makes life interesting.[29]

It makes life interesting for those watching his career, too.

Chapter 10

New Steps

It was spring, 1979. Baryshnikov was on his way to New Haven, Connecticut, to receive an honorary doctorate in fine arts from Yale University. Intense fog diverted his plane, and the pilot was forced to land miles away. A police escort rushed Baryshnikov to the campus, where he arrived just in time to hear the university's president, A. Bartlett Giamatti, declare to the crowd:

> You have brought classical dance to millions as you made your *grands jetés* into their lives. With the courage of your conviction that artistic growth demands adventure, you have dared to let "push come to shove" as you moved from Petipa to Tharp and Balanchine.[30]

This is the legacy of Mikhail Baryshnikov: a lifelong conviction that artistry and adventure go hand in hand. This is how he will be remembered.

A Role Model

In many ways, Mikhail Baryshnikov is a role model. From the beginning, he focused intently on his chosen career. He dedicated his life to being the best in his field. As a dancer-in-training, he took advantage of all the opportunities that came his way. Even in a restrictive society like the Soviet Union, he made sure that he learned all he could. Now, as a world-famous performer, he takes chances with new work and new choreographers, even if their success is not guaranteed.

Baryshnikov's desire for new opportunities continues to this day, as he experiments with ventures outside the world of dance. He is always ready for new challenges, realizing that they are the key to personal satisfaction. All of these attributes are important in defining the man behind the legend.

Other, less favorable aspects of Baryshnikov's personality are occasionally mentioned in the media. He is known to be moody, difficult to work with, an intense perfectionist, and even inconsiderate at times. He admits this, but he has also learned to ignore the media attention. He appreciates time to himself, away from the public eye. He is an avid reader of literature and poetry and enjoys relaxing in his country house outside New York City. Relationships have brought both happiness and sadness to Misha, who has dated many but loved few women. He does not easily find contentment or real happiness.

Baryshnikov's diverse projects are his greatest legacies to the future. His commitment to artistic growth and his remarkable performances inspire all who watch him. By demonstrating that dance is an athletic and powerful activity, he has caught the attention of those who were previously not interested. Because of Baryshnikov, people of all ages have come to love the art of the dance. This is one of his most important contributions to our society.

In addition, Baryshnikov has broken many stereotypes of dancers and dancing. Most significant, he has changed the image of the *male* dancer. Before Baryshnikov's phenomenal entrance onto the American stage, men who chose careers in dance were often ridiculed. In some circles, ballet was not considered a "masculine" or a "strong" profession. Misha helped to change that, with his undeniable strength, athletic body, and sensational technique. Because of Baryshnikov's example, future male dancers may receive greater respect for their career choice.

Baryshnikov has also raised the standards by which ballet dancing is judged. Future *danseurs* will undoubtedly be compared to him, whether it is in the height of their leaps, their

Always moving forward . . . (AP/Wide World Photos)

number of rotations in the air, or the drama behind their expressions. Clearly, Baryshnikov is a hard act to follow.

New Issues

Both personally and professionally, Baryshnikov continues to face new issues. His homeland has undergone radical changes since he left. The Cold War has ended, making way for greater peace between the Soviet Union and the United States. The Soviet people have spoken out against communism and have expressed a desire for a more democratic way of life. Symbolic of this is the renaming of the city of Leningrad to St. Petersburg, as it was originally called. Baryshnikov may decide to return to Russia someday, to revisit the places of his childhood or even to perform again on the stages he once knew so well.

Baryshnikov is also very much aware of another, less hopeful issue which crosses all geographic boundaries: AIDS. AIDS has claimed the lives of many dancers, musicians, actors, and artists. The disease has killed numerous dancers with whom Misha himself worked at American Ballet Theatre. As Artistic Director of ABT, Baryshnikov realized that the toll this deadly illness has taken on his own world of ballet could not be ignored.

Along with other leading figures in dance, Misha has helped make a difference in the battle against AIDS. In 1987, he acted as host at an unprecedented benefit concert called "Dancing for Life" at the New York State Theatre. Thirteen dance groups were present, including ABT, the New York City Ballet, the Paul Taylor and Mark Morris dance companies, and many more—all sharing the same stage. The dancers came together to show the need for action against the common threat of death and to do the one thing that for them means life: dance. Almost three thousand tickets were sold, raising a total of $1.4 million for AIDS research.

Baryshnikov made another contribution to this cause by
publishing a book for adults entitled *The Swan Prince*, based
on the fairy-tale story of *Swan Lake*. It is a lighthearted
take-off on a classic tale in which swans turn into people and
find their fates tragically twisted. Baryshnikov's humorous
version was co-written by choreographer Peter Anastos and
contained photographs by fashion photographer Arthur Elgort.
Baryshnikov's profits from *The Swan Prince* were donated to
AIDS research.

New Adventures

In the early 1990's, Baryshnikov again faced new decisions
concerning his own career. The young man from Riga had
come a long way: from the Kirov Ballet to American Ballet
Theatre; from Balanchine to Broadway; from performer to
director; from ballet dance to modern dance, tap dance to jazz
dance. In an autobiographical videotape called *The Dancer
and the Dance*, Misha revealed his greatest wish and his
greatest conflict:

> I would like to do everything. This country has a lot of
> opportunities. . . . You have so many chances to express yourself.
> Time is my biggest problem. [31]

Misha's schedule of daily ballet class, rehearsals, and travel
leaves little time to spare. Yet time is also a problem in another
way: It is impossible to remain forever in the top physical
condition that is so necessary to dance technique. The aging
process is especially challenging for those whose lives focus
on physical excellence, including dancers and athletes. In his
forties, Baryshnikov faced this issue head-on. He had to cope
with overstressed joints and ankles, as well as several serious
injuries to his knees. (The knee problems required three
surgeries and intensive physical therapy.) Characteristically,
Misha responded to the problems of time and aging by

undertaking a distinctly new adventure.

He added yet another new title to his long list of roles: entrepreneur. In the late 1980's, he entered the cosmetic and fashion industries and became directly involved in the creation of two perfumes, overseeing the development of the scents as well as their marketing and advertising. "Misha" is his perfume for women; "Baryshnikov Pour Homme" is his fragrance for men. He also created a collection of sportswear and dancewear, called "Baryshnikov Bodywear," which is sold in major stores throughout the the United States.

Baryshnikov would actively promote these products himself. A series of slick advertising photographs showing him in exotic locations (at the beach, on a motorcycle, in a café) were shot by famous photographer Annie Leibovitz. Baryshnikov also appeared in stores to sign autographs and chat with customers. He used the profits from his merchandise to support his modern dance company, the White Oak Dance Project, and its tours.

Stay Tuned

Retail merchandising was another outlet for Baryshnikov's creative personality, but his spectacular performances are what will be remembered throughout history. Classical ballets, contemporary ballets, modern dance, motion pictures, television, and theater have all felt the impact of one of the greatest performers of our time. Mikhail Baryshnikov is a dancer, choreographer, director, businessman, father, and friend.

Baryshnikov will be remembered for sharing his flawless Russian ballet training with the West, and for eagerly embracing uniquely American traditions like Broadway. He will be remembered for pushing the limits. His desire for challenge continuously takes him into new territory, resulting in a treasury of inspirational work. Knowing this, his career seems far from over. Indeed, one Los Angeles critic made this observation: "Obviously there's a lot that Mikhail Baryshnikov can do for dance while he still has the world's attention."[32] The final act is yet to come.

First Performances

Vestris, **1969, International Ballet Competition, Moscow.** Leonid Jacobson choreographed this piece for Baryshnikov, who used it to win the gold medal at this competition. The ballet is a series of vignettes that allow Baryshnikov to show off his mimetic and dramatic skills. Baryshnikov reprised the role at American Ballet Theatre in 1975.

Giselle, **January, 1972, Kirov Ballet, Leningrad.** The ballet is an example of a Romantic ballet in the nineteenth century tradition. Baryshnikov portrayed Albrecht, one of the most demanding of the male roles in all of the classical ballets. Portraying Albrecht represents the achievement of an advanced level of skill. This was also the role in which Baryshnikov made his American debut in 1974.

Don Quixote, **August, 1974, American Ballet Theatre, New York City.** Although this was the first full-length ballet that Baryshnikov performed in the Soviet Union, he performed the well-known *grand pas de deux* on its own for American Ballet Theatre. This *pas de deux* (duet) is the classical dancer's ultimate exercise in virtuosity, performed by Baryshnikov with ease.

Theme and Variations, **October, 1974, American Ballet Theatre, Washington, D.C.** This was Baryshnikov's first performance of a dance by George Balanchine, one of the greatest twentieth-century choreographers. Baryshnikov admits that it was one of the most difficult ballets he has performed in the West. Baryshnikov later studied intensively with Balanchine, whose ballets are sometimes called "neoclassic."

Push Comes to Shove, **January, 1976, American Ballet Theatre, New York City.** Choreographed by Twyla Tharp for Baryshnikov and ABT, *Push* is an example of a contemporary ballet. As technically demanding as a classical ballet like *Giselle*, this piece proved Baryshnikov's versatility as a dancer and endeared him to audiences.

Drink to Me Only with Thine Eyes, **Fall, 1988, American Ballet Theatre, New York City.** Baryshnikov, at this time Artistic Director of American Ballet Theatre, invited choreographer Mark Morris to create this contemporary ballet for the company. In this ensemble piece, Baryshnikov was just "one of the gang." A fresh choreographic approach challenged Baryshnikov and made him eager to continue working with Morris.

***El Penitente*, October, 1991, Martha Graham Dance Company, New York City.** Baryshnikov portrayed the title character in this memorable dramatic work by the legendary modern-dance pioneer Martha Graham. He first performed a Graham piece in 1987, and he was so inspired by her method that he went on to study with her in depth. Baryshnikov later adopted *El Penitente* into the repertory of his White Oak Dance Project.

Time Line

1948	*January 27*. Baryshnikov is born in Riga, Latvia.
1960-1964	Studies classical ballet dance at the Riga Dance School.
1964	*September*. Moves to Leningrad to study dance with Alexander Pushkin at the Vaganova Choreographic Institute.
1967	*June*. Stars in a graduation performance (the *pas de deux* from *Don Quixote*) upon graduating from the Vaganova Choreographic Institute.
1967-1974	Performs as a principal dancer with the Kirov Ballet, Leningrad.
1969	Wins a gold medal at the International Ballet Competition in Moscow for his performance in *Vestris*.
1972	*January*. First performs the role of Albrecht in *Giselle*.
1974	*February*. Baryshnikov's "creative evening" at the Kirov: *Daphnis et Chloë*, *Ballet Divertissement*, and *The Prodigal Son*.
1974	*April 20*. Last performance in Russia: *Giselle*, with Natalia Bessmertnova.
1974	*June 29*. Requests political asylum in Montreal, Canada, after a performance with a Soviet touring group.
1974	*July 27*. American debut performance: *Giselle*, with Natalia Makarova and American Ballet Theatre, New York City.
1974-1978	Performs as the principal dancer with American Ballet Theatre.
1976	*January 9*. Premiere of *Push Comes to Shove*, choreographed by Twyla Tharp, American Ballet Theatre, New York City.
1977	*November*. Release of *The Turning Point* (motion picture), directed by Herbert Ross.
1977	*December*. Premiere of Baryshnikov's production of *The Nutcracker* for American Ballet Theatre; also televised by ABC-TV.
1978	*March*. Premiere of Baryshnikov's production of *Don Quixote* for American Ballet Theatre.

1978	*Fall.* Moves from American Ballet Theatre to the New York City Ballet, in order to work with George Balanchine and Jerome Robbins.
1978	*November 14.* Opens New York City Ballet's season in Balanchine's *Rubies.*
1979	*Spring.* Receives an honorary doctorate from Yale University.
1979	*October.* Resigns from New York City Ballet.
1980	*April 24. IBM Presents Baryshnikov on Broadway* is aired on ABC-TV. With Liza Minnelli; choreographed by Ron Field.
1980	*September 1.* Becomes Artistic Director of American Ballet Theatre.
1983	*December 20.* Premiere of *Cinderella,* choreographed by Baryshnikov and Peter Anastos for American Ballet Theatre.
1984	"Baryshnikov by Tharp" is aired on PBS's *Great Performances.* Produced by Don Mischer and Twyla Tharp.
1985	*Summer.* First tour by Baryshnikov and Company, a showcase group from American Ballet Theatre.
1985	*November.* Release of *White Nights* (motion picture), directed by Taylor Hackford.
1987	Introduction of "Baryshnikov Bodywear" to retail stores.
1987	*Fall.* Appears with the Martha Graham Dance Company for the first time.
1987	*October 5.* Host of *Dancing for Life,* a benefit for AIDS research in New York City.
1987	*October.* Release of *Dancers* (motion picture), directed by Herbert Ross.
1988	*December 2.* Premiere of Baryshnikov's production of *Swan Lake* for American Ballet Theatre.
1989	Launch of women's cologne, "Misha."
1989	*February.* Theatrical debut in Kafka's *The Metamorphosis,* at Duke University in North Carolina, followed by a run on Broadway.
1989	*June.* Announces his resignation as Artistic Director of American Ballet Theatre, effective summer, 1990.

1989	*September 28.* Resigns as Artistic Director at American Ballet Theatre months earlier than he had originally planned.
1989	*Fall.* Appears with Mark Morris' Monnaie Dance Group for the first time, in Brussels, Belgium.
1990	*July-August.* Organizes the White Oak Dance Project with Mark Morris in Jacksonville, Florida.
1990	*September.* Release of *Company Business* (motion picture), directed by Nicholas Meyer.
1990	*October 24.* First performance by the White Oak Dance Project in Boston.
1991	Launch of men's cologne, "Baryshnikov Pour Homme."

Notes

Note: *Full bibliographic information is listed in the Bibliography.*

1. Fraser, Private View, p. 237.
2. Baryshnikov, *Baryshnikov at Work*, p. 10.
3. Baryshnikov, *Baryshnikov at Work*, p. 8.
4. Baryshnikov, *Baryshnikov at Work*, p. 9.
5. Baryshnikov, *Baryshnikov at Work*, p. 8.
6. Smakov, *Baryshnikov*, p. 90.
7. Smakov, *Baryshnikov*, p. 92.
8. Smakov, *Baryshnikov*, p. 96.
9. Marcia Siegel, *Watching the Dance Go By*. Boston, Houghton Mifflin, 1977, p. 4.
10. Siegel, *Watching the Dance Go By*, p. 18.
11. Smakov, *Baryshnikov*, p. 126.
12. France, *Baryshnikov in Color*, p. 7.
13. Baryshnikov, *Baryshnikov at Work*, p. 197.
14. France, *Baryshnikov in Color*, p. 6.
15. France, *Baryshnikov in Color*, p. 7.
16. Walter Terry, "American Ballet Theatre's Russian Invasion," *Saturday Review* 7 (May, 1980), pp. 52-54.
17. William Huck, "Ballet Theatre Minus Baryshnikov," *Los Angeles Times*, Calendar section, March 4, 1990, p. 56.
18. Martha Duffy, "Baryshnikov Remodels the ABT," *Time*, May 4, 1981, pp. 80-81.
19. Collins, "Mikhail Baryshnikov."
20. Anna Kisselgoff, "Baryshnikov Tries Graham's World," *The New York Times*, October 6, 1987, p. C13.
21. Jennifer Dunning, "Martha Graham and Baryshnikov: Dynamics of a Simple Relationship," *The New York Times*, October 14, 1991, p. C13.
22. Jack Anderson, "Words of Beauty and Terror inform a Graham Classic," *The New York Times*, October 1, 1989, p. H8.
23. Susan Reiter, "Baryshnikov Goes Modern with Morris," *Los Angeles Times*, October 24, 1990, p. F1.
24. Reiter, p. F1.
25. Nancy Dalva, "Misha and Mark."
26. Dalva, "Misha and Mark."

27. Reiter, p. F1.
28. Nancy Dalva, "A Metamorphosis Indeed: Baryshnikov's Bug Bit," *Dance Magazine* 63, no. 6 [June, 1989], p. 49.
29. Martin Bernheimer, "Baryshnikov at the Turning Point," *Los Angeles Times*, Calendar section, April 4, 1989, p. 1.
30. Smakov, *Baryshnikov*, p. 225.
31. Harriet Millrose et al., *Baryshnikov: The Dancer and the Dance.*
32. Donna Perlmutter, "White Oak Dance Project," *Dance Magazine*, February, 1992, p. 102.

Glossary

Artsoviet: An official committee of the Soviet government, which determined artistic policy.

Choreographer: The creator of a dance, responsible for arranging or composing the steps and patterns of movement.

Choreography: A dance composed and remembered for presentation on a stage.

Classical ballet: A form of dance that emerged in the nineteenth century. It uses a known "vocabulary" of elegant, graceful steps and gestures to tell a story or suggest an idea.

Composer: A writer of music.

***Corps de ballet*:** French for "body of ballet." The ensemble, or body of dancers, of a ballet company.

Dance: A series of rhythmic and patterned movements of the body, often performed to music.

***Danseur*:** The male classical ballet dancer.

***Danseur noble*:** The romantic leading man in a ballet.

Defect: To leave or abandon a cause or a country in order to embrace another.

Demi-caractère: A character role in a ballet, such as the humorous joke or the mother-in-law; such roles are usually exaggerated or created through the use of mime.

***Divertissement*:** A short balletic interlude, as opposed to a full-length story ballet.

Emploi: A system in the Soviet Union of categorizing a dancer according to the type of role for which he or she seems most suited (such as a romantic lead or a character dancer). This "type casting" is based on the dancer's physical appearance, musculature, and technical abilities.

Jazz dance: A form of dance that became popular in the 1940's and is characterized by bent knees, isolated movements such as rotations of the hips or head, syncopated rhythms, and everyday or popular dance gestures.

Librettist: A writer of the story or plot for a ballet.

Modern dance: A form of dance that grew out of a rebellion against ballet dance in the early twentieth century, characterized by flexed feet and hands, emphasis on movements of the torso, and a use of the entire body to express emotions.

103

Mentor: A guide or counselor.

Neoclassical ballet: A twentieth-century form of ballet that emphasizes form (steps and their execution) over dramatic content.

Pas de deux: A "dance for two," or duet.

Pirouette: A turn on one foot.

Plié: A deep knee bend, often used as preparation for turns, jumps, or leaps.

Repertoire: A collection of dances frequently performed by an individual dancer or company.

Tap dance: A form of dance that evolved from social dance, emphasizing the rhythmic sounds and patterns created by the feet striking the floor with different levels of force and speed.

Turn-out: The outward rotation of the hips, which allows the execution of many ballet positions and steps.

Virtuosity: Skill and strength.

Bibliography

Alovert, Nina. *Baryshnikov in Russia.* New York: Holt, Rinehart and
  Winston, 1984. Alovert, professional dance photographer and longtime
  friend of Baryshnikov, describes the dancer's achievements in Russia
  and her recollections of his defection. For mature readers.
Baryshnikov, Mikhail. *Baryshnikov at Work.* New York: Alfred A. Knopf,
  1976. This valuable reference book, filled with beautiful photographs by
  Martha Swope, contains Baryshnikov's personal reflections on his major
  roles. He describes his approach to individual ballets and his philosophy
  of dance.
Bell, Harriet, ed. *Baryshnikov on Broadway.* New York: Harmony Books,
  1980. With a foreword by dance critic Walter Terry, this volume
  chronicles the making of the television special *IBM Presents
  Baryshnikov on Broadway.* Photographs by Martha Swope show the
  dancer, with partner Liza Minnelli, in rehearsals and on stage in scenes
  from popular Broadway musicals.
Collins, Nancy. "Mikhail Baryshnikov." *Rolling Stone*, October 8, 1987, pp.
  56-60. For mature readers, this in-depth interview with Baryshnikov is
  one of the few he has allowed. He frankly discusses his childhood,
  personal life, and opinions on dance in Russia and America.
Dalva, Nancy. "Misha and Mark: Out on a Limb." *Dance Magazine* 65, no.
  1 (January, 1991), p. 40. Entertaining and informative, this article
  describes the collaboration of Baryshnikov and modern dancer Mark
  Morris as they assembled the White Oak Dance Project. Offers their
  insights into the creative process, as well as descriptions of the dances on
  which they collaborated.
France, Charles, ed. *Baryshnikov in Color.* New York: Harry Abrams, 1980.
  With photographs by Martha Swope and others, this large-size book
  contains an introduction and commentary written by Baryshnikov
  himself. Further insight into the dancer's creative process is provided, as
  well as glorious photographs.
Fraser, John. *Private View: Inside Baryshnikov's American Ballet Theatre.*
  New York: Bantam Books, 1988. With photographs by Eve Arnold, a
  revealing book focused on Baryshnikov's experience as Artistic Director
  of the ballet company (1980-1989). Discusses serious issues and
  problems, such as drug abuse, eating disorders, and AIDS, as well as the
  dancer's successes. For mature readers.

Jowitt, Deborah. "Baryshnikov: His Years at ABT." *Dance Magazine* 64, no. 1 (January, 1990). This lengthy article assesses the strengths and weaknesses of Baryshnikov's tenure as Artistic Director of American Ballet Theatre. A good overview of his accomplishments through 1990.

Makarova, Natalia. *A Dance Autobiography.* New York: Alfred A. Knopf, 1979. Makarova's story of her training, career in Russia, and defection to the West is readable and informative. She frequently refers to Baryshnikov, who was her partner in numerous ballets. Containing many impressive photographs, her autobiography provides insight into their common experiences and the different choices that they made.

Payne, Charles. *American Ballet Theatre.* New York: Alfred A. Knopf, 1978. This elegant picture-book describes the history of ABT. The chapter entitled "The Seventies" includes detailed information about Baryshnikov's defection, first performances, and contributions to the company.

Smakov, Gennady. *Baryshnikov: From Russia to the West.* New York: Farrar Straus Giroux, 1981. For mature readers, this is an intimate biography of Baryshnikov. Smakov, writer and dance critic, is a fellow Russian émigré and friend of the dancer. The book offers a unique perspective on Baryshnikov's life and work in Russia in contrast to his life and work in the United States.

Victor, Thomas. *The Making of a Dance: Mikhail Baryshnikov and Carla Fracci in Medea.* New York: Holt, Rinehart and Winston, 1976. This oversize picture-book (with photographs by the author) tells the story of the creation of a ballet by John Butler. An interesting look at the creative process of choreography and dance production.

Media Resources

Carmen. Video. 1980. Distributed by Kultur. A production of French choreographer Roland Petit's version of the famous ballet, starring Baryshnikov and French ballerina Zizi Jeanmaire.

Golan, Menahme, and Yoram Globus, producers. *Dancers*. Annon Group, 1987. This love story, directed by Herbert Ross, stars Baryshnikov and ballerinas Alessandra Ferri, Leslie Browne, newcomer Julie Kent, and members of American Ballet Theatre. The plot revolves around a ballet company preparing for a performance of *Giselle*.

Hackford, Taylor, and William S. Gilmore, producers. *White Nights*. Columbia Pictures, 1985. Starring Baryshnikov and preeminent tap dancer and actor Gregory Hines, this thriller revolves around an American tap dancer and a Russian ballet dancer. Thrown together, they fight against the Soviet government as the worlds of dance and politics collide. The film contains exuberant dance sequences choreographed by Twyla Tharp.

Hemion, Dwight, and Gary Smith, producers. *IBM Presents Baryshnikov on Broadway*. ABC-TV, 1981. With choreography by Ron Field, Baryshnikov and partner Liza Minnelli present song-and-dance scenes from popular Broadway musicals, including *Oklahoma*, *Guys and Dolls*, and *A Chorus Line*.

Jaffe, Steven-Charles, producer. *Company Business*. Metro-Goldwyn-Mayer, 1991. Stars Baryshnikov and Gene Hackman, who play spies who form an unlikely alliance against political villains.

Large, Brian, director. *Don Quixote*. Part of the *Great Performances* series. Public Broadcasting Service, 1984. Baryshnikov, who choreographed this version of the classical ballet, is also its star. Also with Cynthia Harvey and Patrick Bissell.

Millrose, Harriet, and Victor Millrose, producers, in association with Melvin Bragg. *Baryshnikov: The Dancer and the Dance*. Video. Directed by Tony Cash. London Weekend Television, 1983. Distributed by Kultur. Narrated by actress Shirley MacLaine, this intimate profile of Baryshnikov features his reflections on his childhood, training, and career. The video also illustrates the artistic process, as American Ballet Theatre rehearses and then performs a new ballet choreographed by Choo San Goh.

Mischer, Don, and Twyla Tharp, producers. "Baryshnikov by Tharp." Part of the *Dance in America* series. Alexandria, Va.: Public Broadcasting Service, 1984. Baryshnikov hosts this program, which features the dancer in roles created by Tharp. Excerpts from *Push Comes to Shove* and *Sinatra Suite* are included, as well as Baryshnikov's reminiscences of his childhood and training.

The Nutcracker. CBS Television, 1977. This version of the holiday classic is choreographed by Baryshnikov and danced by American Ballet Theatre. Baryshnikov plays the Prince, Gelsey Kirkland plays Clara, and Alexander Minz plays Drosselmeyer.

Public Broadcasting Service. "Baryshnikov at Wolf Trap." Part of the *In Performance at Wolf Trap* series. Public Broadcasting Service, 1976. Distributed by Kultur. Baryshnikov's American television debut was aired shortly after he had defected from the Soviet Union. He performs the solo *Vestris*, as well as excerpts from *Don Quixote* with partner Gelsey Kirkland.

Ross, Herbert, and Arthur Laurents, producers. *The Turning Point.* Twentieth Century-Fox, 1977. This popular film about life and love backstage at the ballet stars Anne Bancroft, Shirley MacLaine, and real-life ballerina Leslie Browne. Baryshnikov was nominated for an Academy Award for his portrayal of Yuri Kopeikin. Features wonderful dance segments performed by Baryshnikov and American Ballet Theatre.

The Arts

MIKHAIL BARYSHNIKOV

INDEX